TABITHA D. JAMES

S.H.E. thought She could, so She did.

Not Posted:
S.E.A.S.O.N.S. of the Untold

a motivational memoir

Composed By:
Tabitha D. James

All rights reserved. No portion of this book may be reproduced in any form without permission from the publisher, except as permitted by U.S. copyright law.

For permissions contact:
1 Am She
ATTN: Tabitha D. James
P.O. Box 82
Lake View, SC 29563
empoweringtoday@1amshe.com

This book is a work of fiction with the exception of personal excerpts. Names, characters, places, and incidents are products of the author's imagination or are used fictitiously. Any resemblance to actual persons, living or dead, events, or locales is entirely coincidental.

Cover by ExKlusive Kreations

Copyright © 2017 Tabitha D. James
1 Am She, LLC

First Printing: July 2017

All rights reserved.

ISBN-13: 978-0-692-90993-5

DEDICATION

"I KNEW I could because she believed I could."
There are no words to describe my humble gratefulness for a mother who has never doubted my dreams. Truly grateful! In our struggle, I found my strength and the rest was history.

To my "village", you are indeed a miracle, you've molded and shaped me to be all I could have ever imagined and more; from the bottom of my heart, thank you!

To you -yes you- the one currently reading this, thank you for your support; it means more than I can actually express. Enjoy ☺

CONTENTS

	FORWARD	i
1	Strength	1
2	Endurance	7
3	Attitude	13
4	Sacrifice	19
5	Optimism	26
6	Neglect	32
7	Social Perception **(Bonus)**	39
	S.E.A.S.O.N.S.	44
	Conclusion : Until We Meet Again	45

FOREWARD

This book was never intended to incorporate so much about self, however as I began to tour the country and share bits of my story, the vision began to unfold. As you journey through the S.E.A.S.O.N.S. presented in these chapters, you will conclude with a sense of the Not. Posted. And it is intended that you will have the motivation to empower by the untold.

It is my ultimate hope as the "composer" of this memoir that you finish this book empowered to reflect on the untold or "not. posted" aspect of your own life. How can it empower others? Better yet, how can you use it to empower yourself? Despite your battle , it is inevitable that we have all overcome something in life. We cannot ever erase our past however we can grab a new sheet of paper to write out, sketch out and plan out the future. Be inspired!

Oh, and, this is as authentic as it gets. There were no major edits to this as it is an original memoir, from my desk to the printer. You may see a typo, you may even catch a misspelled word and that is okay. We can't always edit and filter everything, this is to capture the . . . .

Not. Posted

1 STRENGTH

THE QUALITY OR STATE OF BEING STRONG, IN PARTICULAR.
A GOOD OR BENEFICIAL QUALITY OR ATTIRBUTE.

Imagine the strongest person you know? Why do you believe that they are strong? What stands out about their strength? Do you now have a person in mind? If so, great; if not keep thinking before you go on! Now imagine yourself in their situation. Can you even imagine such a thing? Do you even really know their situation or do you only know the filtered version that has helped you to develop a perception that may or may not be accurate.

There isn't necessarily an accurate way to get an "inside scoop" on someone's story or the magnitude of their strength unless you actually get to know them. Even once you get to know them, a certain level of trust has to be developed for one to breakdown the barrier for sharing stories. It is human nature for us to judge based on the "posted" or perceived nature of one's life.

Even before social media, there was a saying "what happens in this house, stays in this house" that blocked the revealing of "real truths". This saying and the like have subconsciously made people develop a sense of strength, or dealing, through silence. Issues plaguing the family such as outside children, mental illness, financial hardship, rape and the list goes on, all silenced by "what happens in this house, stays in this house". Though highly unlikely, maybe you haven't experienced any of the previous scenarios. In the case that you haven't, I'm willing to bet that if someone close to you will disclose the unfiltered story of the past, you have been directly or indirectly impacted by such a situation as exemplified. How do I know? Well it is highly unlikely that throughout the duration of your family's existence that every person was 100% honest about all the situations that occurred. Many families however are better at keeping the "real truths" hidden to protect the peace of those around them. Though this may seem decent and beneficial on the surface, it can potentially have a negative impact in the long run.

Despite the negative aspects of hiding pertinent information and shameful situations, it definitely builds a sense of subconscious strength because not only do the affected have to deal with the situation, they must also deal with the secrecy around the situations. Take for example the child that was wrongfully abused – physically, sexually, or mentally – by someone who was deemed trustable. Over years this child must grow, this same child may grow to have trust issues or built anger as a subconscious reaction to a situation from their hidden past. Maybe that young girl or boy could never find the strength to "tattle-tell" or just maybe they tried to tell but was ignored or called a liar because hey, Uncle Leroy would never do such a thing. And dear heavens not Aunt Sherry, she's too saved for anything of such nature as rape or verbal abuse to occur in her household.

Twenty, thirty, forty years later, that same child may have never gained the strength to overcome what happened all those years ago. Their children have suffered, their spouse has suffered, their colleagues are bothered by their never ceasing sense of anger, the neighbors are wondering why they never speak pleasantly or wave with a smile. All of these people impacted for years just because "what happens in this house, stays in this house". Strength has been acquired in an abnormal sense of defense, a sense of anger, a sense of blockage. The abuser was never forgiven nor forgotten.

Hopefully this scenario isn't your life or that of anyone close to you; however if in fact it is, I am requesting that you forgive. Find the strength to forgive the person that doesn't even know to say sorry. Releasing the anger, the guilt and the bottled up emotion will help alleviate the pain. Easy? No, now I did not say that, I just simply said do it – find the inner strength.

On the reverse, maybe this scenario isn't your story. Great! I wouldn't wish it on anyone. I do ask for you to find a sliver of patience with others for situations such as exemplified are very common. Many we interact with on a daily basis are fighting battles of which aren't posted, aren't discussed and have never been acknowledged. Before you flip, before you judge, before you form a preconceived notion, take a moment to reflect. The not . posted, unfiltered person may be missing the strength of overcoming past experiences. Is this an excuse for unpleasant behaviors? Well not really, however it is simply one of the reasons why many are uneasy, always bitter and all around displeasing to interact with. Their strength is sourced from a place of defensing mechanisms opposed to defeating mechanisms.

Get to know your surroundings and things such as this will become much easier to pinpoint. We are often attracted to develop friendships and relationships with people whom we connect with on the surface. I find that the most healthy connections are those that are intentional, transparent and genuine. The ones where a filter is not needed. The YOU that YOU are is openly exposed and unashamed. It takes pure strength to even form such relationships. Often times even those you've known the longest, have no idea what you've been through or experienced. They know what you've chosen to share.

Now, don't think I am preaching for you to become an open book. Not by any means is that where this is going however just try releasing a piece of you that is not. posted. You'll realize quick that the "not . posted" alignment has very little to do with social media. Depending on age, life alignment and other demographics, social media not even play a factor in your life directly. Not . Posted speaks to the you that nobody knows but YOU. The you that may be of help or hindrance to self and others if not handled properly.

The strength in accepting you for you is step one to much greatness. Not professional greatness, not educational greatness, but intrinsic greatness. The type of greatness that empowers you to be a better you for yourself and your family. Oh Tab, how do you know? Uh, I thought you'd never ask . . . Well when weak isn't an option one finds strength -period-.

NOT POSTED

A GLIMPSE OF THE UNTOLD: STRENGTH

People's perception of you is formed based on when they met you – thus stating, if you meet someone strong, it's automatically assumed they've always been strong. As a mentor, a motivator, a person of high enthusiasm it is often perceived that I just popped out the womb happy. Hmmm… I'm sure I was smiling but life had its twists and turns to aid the development of true strength. What happens in this house, stays in this house . . . Haunting words as I reflect over my life and piece together the various situations where protecting piece ruined my judgement, my perception, my overall understanding.

From being sheltered from certain family members to being denied true identity basically being persuaded that I was someone I was not, all aided in the development of subconscious strength. In the season of subconscious strength, I resorted to outside acceptance as a form of relief. The urge to be liked, to be acknowledged by any and all means. This meant doing things both seen and unseen that never correlated with my true character but were an anesthetic for the pain.

It wasn't until I did just what was suggested earlier, practiced forgiveness, that I found real strength. Strength to move on in spite of, strength to accept whatever was thrown my way, strength to say "I shall not be defeated". Forgiving meant accepting apologies that were never given. It meant being grudge-free. Parents, family members, friends of family – all having to be forgiven for imaginary apologies. Never realizing that the strength was being built as I was merely surviving. So many times giving up seemed easier, and by giving up I don't mean dropping out, nor quitting; I am relating this to the ultimate escape. Feeling that I wasn't strong enough to stay; it would be much easier without me. Feeling as if I was a nuisance. I'm still not sure what happened, I think I was too scared to harm myself or maybe I knew the devastation it would cause for my mother. Whatever it was, I am glad it blocked the thought. Still here!

The season of acquiring strength was long, in fact it's ever evolving. I share this to say to you, forgive, move on, keep pushing. Someone may have hurt you, hit you, abandoned you – accept the apology that has yet to come and tap into your season of strength. On the other spectrum, maybe you've been striving towards a certain dream and experienced defeat after defeat. Allow that defeat to fuel you not define you; keep pushing . . .

"If you're defined by your weakness, you're allowing whatever has temporary control to ultimately win. You're defeated. If you're instead defined by your strength, you're confirming power over your life. You're victorious."

2 ENDURANCE
THE FACT OR POWER OF ENDURING AN UNPLEASANT OR DIFFICULT PROCESS OR SITUATION WITHOUT GIVING WAY.

Okay, we're stronger, we are claiming strength over our lives, our situations and our connections. Can we now endure? Often in workouts and training you hear about strength and endurance simultaneously. In training, the athlete's strength is measured by how strong they are. How much can they lift? How heavy can the load be?

Endurance on the other hand, how long can you go? How many laps can you run? How many repetitions before a break? Mastery of the two simultaneously is quite the craft.

Imagine yourself and your situation as the athlete. You have a heavy load, burdens, break-ups, past experiences, current challenges and fears of the future all at once. Now, you're faced with a test of endurance. How long can you carry all these without breaking? Without bending? Without completely throwing in the towel?

No downplay to strength as it is a key virtue for life; however what is strength if you can't carry the load as long as it takes? If you can only be strong for a moment, how valuable is your strength? If your strength is only for the moment and not for the mile, it's time to shift the training session. Some endurance is needed to see it through.

Similar to strength, we don't wake up being enduring creatures. Actually, we are developed with a very low sense of actual endurance. It is the life experiences that shape the varying levels of endurance. For some endurance is tested early. The child who has to endure several surgeries to merely survive beyond infancy. This is an early introduction to the realm of endurance. The toddler forced into systematic care at no fault of their own; another early introduction. The child or teen that has to witness consistent abuse, violence or the similar. Yet another premature introduction. As a youthful person, the realization that endurance is being created isn't even a thought. The mind isn't quite developed enough to conceptualize with what is happening.

The young adult facing the challenges of life head-on. Seeking higher education, establishing in life, finding a sense of self – all require endurance. None of these are overnight processes, thus stating, one has to see it through. The issue with endurance is , plainly enough, many just don't grasp it. Before the breakthrough can come, the give up occurs. It got too hard, the results weren't as expected, the going got tough. Excuses are endless.

The parent raising difficult children, the caregiver seeing after an elderly family member, the employee who feels it is time for promotion however promotion has yet to come. The examples that shape levels of endurance are endless. I could go on and on however I'm sure you have the point. Now if you will, take a moment to self-reflect. How much are willing to endure? Can you recall a situation where you had to endure something unfair or unfamiliar to achieve, to live, to thrive? How did it go? What was the outcome?

As you continue to reflect, imagine situations in which endurance isn't an option but a requirement for survival. The situation you are currently reflecting upon may be one that fits into the category of "no choice, I had to". If so, I commend you. Not to discredit those of you who can't relate in this very moment, but to empower and respect those who achieved endurance by default.

If you travel back to the same house where "what happens stays", that child who was abused, misused, cursed or worse, had to endure. It wasn't a choice of endurance , it was a choice of survival. A forced reaction to the situation of which they were placed into at no control of their own. There is something very special that can be learned from these folks. It. Is. Possible.

Maybe you want to move from your current location. Possibly you are seeking a promotion or a new job. Just maybe you want to upgrade your life holistically. Yearning to make a difference for yourself, your children, your family. Take note from those who have had to endure as a sense of survival. It. Is. Possible. You may have to endure some sacrifices, something we will talk about a little later in this piece. You may have to shift your thought process or even alter your surroundings. Whatever it is that you have to do, endure!

Your ability to see it through will be a true measurement of where you go, what you do and how you overcome. Despite age, gender, race, etc. you have a story. You have had to endure something already, just think about it. Well, if you're reading this – you made it through – Congratulations!

A GLIMPSE OF THE UNTOLD: ENDURANCE

Tiny Tab, what do you know about endurance? Your life is pretty amazing – young, successful, fulfilling your destiny. Well as all that may be true, I must attest that had I not found a strong sense of endurance, none and I mean NONE of the things I have achieved would have been possible.

As a young child, my mother became ill and life as I knew it turned upside down. Seemingly it was from first class to what class, from the top to the bottom, so I thought at that time. My parents separated, I was moved around several times and everyday seemed like a battle between why and how. By the age of 10, I had in my mind that if at all in my power, my mother and I would be okay one day. I did not know how at that time but I found some sense of endurance.

Having to live and deal with family members was a blessing and a curse. A true test of premature endurance. Not to say I was mistreated because that wouldn't be 100% true; however I was not treated as I had been used to so as a child, I had absolutely no idea how to receive what was happening. In 2003, my mother became stable enough for us to live on our own. I prayed, " may we never have to live with anyone else again" . Somehow,

God answered those prayers – through endurance. There were several times I should have reached out for help, but being afraid that things would turn into a whirlwind so I remained silent. I dealt with things the best way I knew how.

Learning how to manage finances, shop for the home, make decisions and so forth became second nature all before sweet 16. Was it easy? Not nearly. However it seemed better than any other option. It wasn't until a near death experience that I finally called a cry for help. Though I was the one to rush my mother to the hospital, I called others for support and assistance. Made it through that situation and kept going. All of these things were happening as I was still a scholar, still an athlete and still a "lover" to someone.

Talk about endurance – not knowing then or even realizing how supernatural the ability to make it had come. It was my normal, I saw nothing special about it, I just knew I did not want to be separated from my mother or our home again. Even in my decision to pursue higher education, without a doubt I was not going too far as I knew my responsibility.

Working full-time, often well exceeding 60 hours per week, to ensure that my mother nor I ever had to worry about finances. Enduring long hours, restless nights and times when I just felt it would be better to let go . . .See that's the part **Not . Posted**. Everyone saw the cheer, the joy, the awards, the accolades; most people, even those close to me never knew when I was at my wits end. The art of endurance had covered me so that I was silent and became masked with a costume of excellence.

Looking back, I am grateful for the trials and tribulations as crazy as it may sound. Now, the small things do not even get much attention. The ability to endure such issues that make you question your life and ability to press through allot for you to be able to shift small things out of the mind. There are bigger fish to fry, bigger mountains to move and more magic to make.

"May you be empowered with a sense of endurance that allows you to overcome any and all situations that were designed to bump you, shake you or even break you . . .You win"

3 ATTITUDE

A SETTLED WAY OF THINKING OR FEELING ABOUT SOMEONE OR SOMETHING, TYPICALLY ONE THAT IS REFLECTED IN A PERSON'S BEHAVIOR.

We've found our strength, we've measured our endurance now what about that attitude. What in the world does attitude have to do with what we were just discussing . . . . Oh my friend , attitude makes all the difference. Attitude alters not only how you react but also how you process the process.

Let's go back to our child from the "what happens in this house, stays in this house" environment. The child is now a teen who has had his or her secret situation bottled up inside for 10 or more years by now. It would be very hard to believe that the bottled up feelings would not be reflected in attitude. The child may be reluctant to change or easily angered or untrustworthy. These characteristics could likely be linked to the reaction of the events that have never been talked about or acknowledged.

Since the child is never allotted the opportunity to talk, to release, to reveal – their attitude is impacted. For some it is teeth sucking, eye-rolling and disrespect. For some it is bashfulness, silence and distant ways. Regardless of how the energy is exerted, unsolved problems area classified by some sort of natural reaction.

If the child grows up without the chance to address any issues, the issues don't disappear. Unless there is a structured process to aid in healing, the now adult may have attitude issues that are directly linked to their untold story from childhood issues. Just as you may have unhealed pieces, so might those that you interact with on a daily basis. As previously stated, I want you to really utilize this memoir has an opportunity to expand your thoughts, your judgments and your reactions.

We all know a Bitter Betty, Terrible Tommy, Nasty Nancy, Cussing Chris and the infamous Debbie Downer. It is my hope that you aren't one of these, but if you are I do pray for the adjustment and alignment for happier days and thoughts. If you aren't one of these, I am willing to bet that you know someone who directly aligns with these fictional characters.

Bitter Betty, who no matter what, her attitude never changes, she is always upset, always speaking negatively about others and always complaining. Terrible Tommy, he acted out his whole childhood and grew up to be in and out of the system. Nasty Nancy, who not only has a nasty attitude but her overall persona just makes everybody she comes in contact with wonder if she ever wakes up on the right side of the bed. Cussing Chris, one would think he/she doesn't know many more words beyond profanity. Lastly, our favorite, the most infamous, Debbie Downer. Debbie doesn't believe anything positive is possible. If you want your dream killed, bring it on to Debbie and she will shoot it down with no issues. It is almost definite to believe that Debbie hasn't said anything uplifting or positive in years.

Are you laughing right now because you can relate someone in your direct or indirect life circle to one of those characters? Are you wondering where is this going with attitude? Let's continue on!

Our attitudes play a huge role in life. They affect how we act and react. How people perceive us and classify us. Those characters are classified solely by the attitude they chose to display. What attitude do you choose when you wake up in the mornings? Did you know that you choose an attitude? Yes, you choose your attitude.

It's 8:30AM, you wake up, you're running late and need to be in the office by 9:15AM for a meeting. You rush rush rush to get ready and out the door. You spill hot coffee in the car and are about .5 inches from a minor accident while turning into the parking lot. As you park and run inside, you have time to choose the attitude you take into the meeting. You have the option to shake it off and walk in with a positive attitude to have an amazing day. You also have an option to walk in complaining about the alarm not going off, the coffee spilling or the accident that did not even occur. The responsive attitude is yours to choose. What do you do?

Life itself is 10% what happens to us and 90% how we choose to respond. The attitude we chose to bring impacts our altitude. The most difficult part about the 90% is those things we chatted about earlier that impact our mindset. It may seem crazy, but I invite you to join me in the research. Our past experiences and how we dealt or did not deal with them have an impact on our daily mind, processing and attitude selection. Bitter Betty may be so damaged by her untold story or stories that she doesn't even realize how her bitterness is effecting how people perceive her. She honestly have transitioned into a state of not caring. Have you heard "I don't care what they think, they better deal with it"? A chosen attitude. Yes, we all deserve individuality and opinion but when it is at the cost of others and true well-being, attitude adjustment is needed.

Referring to the definition of attitude -- a **settled** way of thinking or feeling about someone or something – Betty has **settled** with a bitter attitude towards life. Debbie has **settled** with a downer attitude. How can it be adjusted? Sometimes it never changes. Sometimes life's experiences align and adjustment occurs. The saddest situations are when people similar to our fictional characters never experience attitude adjustment. Going through life for years and years carry those burdens of negative experiences through negative attitudes and actions. Despite your age while reading this, don't let this be you . . Let go . . Whatever happened in that house and stayed in that house, let it go.

Allowing past experiences, rather the past means 15 minutes ago or 15 years ago, to hinder you your mind, your attitude, your thought process is detrimental. Let it go . . .

A GLIMPSE OF THE UNTOLD: ATTITUDE

Not really sure where to start or stop with this attitude portion. For many years, I was classified as having a terrible attitude. With peers, teachers, family members, basically anyone who decided they wanted to "cross me". Hindsight is 20/20 so it's actually very insightful to look back on with my current perspective.

In the moment I never thought of my attitude or how it impacted people's perception of me. One reason, I was very young. Despite my untold responsibilities and "adult-like" ways, I was but a child, therefore I acted and responded as such. My attitude was an unheard cry. Instead of someone recognizing the issue and talking to me. I was criticized, ridiculed and placed in a very unrelating category of people who don't see it through.

I'm guessing now that nobody in my direct or indirect path had the capacity to identify what was really wrong. Before the age of 10 I had witnessed more than many do in a lifetime. Confused about what was really happening I was just living through things. It had become my normal. Abuse, not of the physical nature but mentally and emotionally. Being taken from princess to poverty wasn't the easiest transition and it definitely wasn't easy without any explanation. Just being moved and no realistic communication. It was as if there was nothing to say, nothing to discuss and nothing to expose.

Despite my youthful age, I wasn't idiotic, I had been around adults my entire life thus training my mind to observe, to listen, to think beyond my years. Furthermore, I was pretty smart if I must say myself, therefore I was inquisitive, I wanted to know, I wanted to understand what in the world was going on. Do you think someone asked me anything? Nah. Asked how I felt or if I was okay with the things that were happening? Nah. And it's fine, it made me tough, it made me flexible, it me adaptive to unrecognizable situations.

So where does attitude come in? I exerted my energy

though my attitude. When I was tired of wearing the "mask" and drained from trying to live a "normal" life in the midst of chaos, the only way I could respond was through snapping. I would get into arguments and debates with teachers, fights and verbal feuds with my peers. It was my way to release all the things inside. Not sure why or how this became my comforting mechanism but it did. For years, exerting anger as a way to prove myself and my strength.

As an adult, scholar and survivor, I just wonder why nobody paid enough attention to realize what was going on. I was often kicked out of class and suspended a few times however way to academically strong to be kicked out of school indefinitely. Had a middle-school principal say I would never make it out of high school successfully with the way I acted. Yet another adult not seeing that there was more to my anger than meets the eye. As it relates to that gentleman, I hope someone can go tell him about my success. Not to brag, but to simply let him know that was a horrific thing to say to a 12 year old.

I can't quite coin when I began to shift my attitude. It was such a difficult process to bare alone. Being that nobody knew I was damaged, they couldn't really know I was working to heal. As I was aging through the teenage years, I was attempting to shift but at any given moment I would crack. If someone said or did something to trigger my anger, the attitude would attack.

When I left my hometown to attend college, things began to shift a little better. I realized that in order to conquer the world and be ultimately successful, there was no way I could make it with built up anger. I found my faith, not religion, but faith and began to really focus on shifting my attitude. The process was real, the process was trying, the process was painful but the process was necessary. I forgave those who never knew to say sorry. I can never forget the harm that was done however I can live pass it in order to fulfill true destiny.

During the process I couldn't be around certain people from my past. The sight of them was harmful to my well-being and I did not need to tamper with the process. I couldn't go certain places or engage in certain activities; I was intentional in my encounters and choices. I wanted to be a better person, not a bitter person. Bitter Betty nor Nasty Nancy were the identities I wanted to embody. It took work, it took sacrifice, it took devotion, it took patience. As crazy as it sounds, I am so grateful for it. Everybody loves the butterfly, not knowing the journey of the caterpillar.

Shifting my attitude changed my entire life. It was as if I had new eyes, new lips and a new brain. I saw life through a different perspective. I had survived a tough spot. Considered many things during the process to the extent that I wanted to quit at everything including life. When my peers, colleagues and administrators thought I was on high, I was really on low. In my past life, I had perfected the "mask", being able to portray happy was second nature. But I made it – it remained untold and Not . Posted but I made it . . .

"Life doesn't come with a remote, no instructions, no written rules to follow — you have to take control of it for yourself. Your attitude is a small thing yet it makes a huge difference in how you see, receive and believe . ." -Take Control

"Control is taken, now where shall we go, wherever we go let us go with a positive mindset believing that we will make it, we will survive and we will thrive"

"There's beauty in the storm, sweetness in the sacrifice and relief in release. Never hold on to things that are meant to be gone"

4 SACRIFICE
AN ACT OF SLAUGHTERING AN ANIMAL OR PERSON OR SURRENDERING A POSSESSION AS AN OFFERING TO GOD OR TO A DIVINE OR SUPERNATURAL FIGURE.

S.E.A. . . . we've reached the middle of the season, it's time for some talk about sacrifice. Sacrifice has a direct relation to our strength, endurance and attitude. It too can be introduced in premature form and change your whole outlook. Some of you may not be able to relate but when you grow up in any type of poverty, sacrifice is second nature.

For some, sacrifice means your mother went hungry to feed you and your siblings. For others, sacrifice means mother had to choose between the bills and new clothes for you. For many, you had to choose between going to school or going to work or trying to manage the two for survival. These are just a few examples, sacrifice comes in all shapes, sizes and forms. It comes for the young, the old and the in between. It is a part of life. It may not be our favorite part but it is an integral part.

In reality, you cannot achieve anything without some sort of sacrifice. If you want to make more money, you need more training or education, you have to sacrifice. If you want to save more money, you have to spend less meaning you may cut something you once enjoyed to increase your savings account. You want to be better at a hobby, you have to practice, you have to work it. To do so, you must sacrifice your time and energy. I used these basic examples to depict that sacrifice comes, no matter what. Even our child in the "what happens in this house, stays in this house" environment had to sacrifice. Sacrifice of openness to preserve the perception. The magnitude of sacrifice may vary however it comes for you just as it came for me and everyone else.

The shaping that accompanies sacrifice is incomparable. The higher you're working to go, the more sacrifice required. The more you're working to change your family, the more sacrifice required. That new car you want, that new house, that promotion, bring on the sacrifice for without it, your desires aren't truly attainable. They are dreams in the atmosphere.

What happens when the sacrifice required for our desires is a person or people? The first thought is, let them go. Sounds easy . . . but what if it's people you love? People who have been in your life for longer than the trail period. What do you do? Well one, you assess your desires. Are they genuine? Are they honorable? If you answered yes based on your value system and it still seems necessary to sacrifice those folks . . . they have to go. It may take time and maybe you do not have to completely block them from your life however you can't give them the time and energy you once did or your desires will remain dreams of the atmosphere.

How many people do you think left this world with their true desires left unfulfilled? Maybe there desires were to merely overcome their past experiences. Plenty "what happens in this house, stays in this house" children grew up and never overcame. Lived a full life with bottled up anger. Not saying these individuals never sacrificed anything, quite sure they did, however since it didn't align with embracing the untold, they left this world with issues left unreleased. Maybe they became successful, maybe they didn't. Possibly they lived a life one would think was amazing but left this world never sacrificing enough to forgive. Happens daily, but since you're reading this, you've taken a step towards this not being you.

I am currently challenging you on two levels of sacrifice. The first level is to sacrifice enough to embrace the untold portion of your life. Now don't read this beyond what I am saying; I am not asking you to reveal it to the world or write about it or speak about it. I am merely asking you to embrace it in whatever way brings peace and ultimate healing for you. Your sacrifice may simply be accepting that you got hurt, you were neglected, you were done wrong or whatever the situation was. You may be able to just think back, accept what happen and move on. That won't work for everyone, maybe someone else needs to talk it out, write a letter to the person who partook in the wrongdoing rather you deliver it or not, the expression through writing can potentially provide healing. Whatever it takes, sacrifice the time and energy to better yourself, your mindset and your well- being.

For my success strivers, sacrifice needs to be your middle name and you'll find out why in just a few minutes. Despite what success may mean to you or what phase of life you're in, without sacrifice your desires are what . . . ? You've got it – dreams of the atmosphere!

A GLIMPSE OF THE UNTOLD: SACRIFICE

Oh the joy of Tiny Tab and sacrifice. As with most things in this little life of mine, I was definitely introduced to sacrifice and survival pretty early. Prior to my mother's extended period of illness, I witnessed her sacrifice time with me to ensure I had all I could ever want or need. She brought something new to me each and every day. While my parents were together, I was treated as royalty and then life changed. The art of sacrifice came and I sure didn't ask for the introduction.

Having to live in someone else's home, sacrifice of personal space. Having to depend on people, sacrifice of independency. Becoming a caregiver, sacrifice of childhood. The list goes on but I won't bore you, I rather encourage you. Each and every one of those sacrifices increased my strength and endurance and it took multiple forms of sacrifice to adjust my attitude. Life revealed that in every season, it was just like the Legos I once played with, it's about building.

Fast forward to overcoming and surviving, it took sacrifice. Growing up I always knew I was going to college, it wasn't an option rather I was or not. the only option was "what college". Well that was amazing to the princess but quite different in poverty. I learned early how finances and money worked, having such knowledge, I knew that on a fixed income my mother would not be able to sustain for both of us while I obtained my degree. I had to sacrifice.

Through both my undergrad and graduate study, I juggled multiple jobs to not only ensure I was okay, but to make sure my mother wanted for nothing. I realized quickly when I entered the workforce in 2009, that my mother had sacrificed so much to try and meet my princess desires even when we were near poverty. Ownership may have been the only thing that really sustained us from ever being dead broke. I sacrificed my time, energy, sleep and overall health in general to not just be successful but to survive. There would be consecutive days when I did not sleep. Work, class, meetings, grab a snack and repeat the drill. Still framed in the mindset of "masking" that most people never really knew the sacrifice.

My peers knew I worked hard, they didn't know how hard or how much. I rarely let people in – did not want to tamper with the "image". It was what I knew, you sacrifice and do what you have to do but it's not to be broadcasted or shared. The mask and sacrifice combined almost drove me crazy. Resorting to unnecessary sex, drugs and alcohol became a coping mechanism. It was an anesthetic to the pain of such high levels of sacrifice. Looking back, I often wonder how I survived, yet I realize it was nothing shy of divine power protecting me for the greatness to come.

After I survived the substance abuse and overcame the need to utilize sexual ability as a way to cope – things became easier to navigate. The sacrifice for ultimate success was still high however my attitude shifted, my level of endurance without unnecessary enhancers allowed for life to flow more abundantly. I began to read and research in order to "work on myself" and it yielded me being able to help others.

I started to sacrifice my time and energy to help others along the way. As crazy as my life was, people trusted and believed in my advice, mostly because they only knew the "masked" person. The sacrifice and struggle weren't worn on my sleeve, the confidence and courage was. It wasn't real at the time, however it was what I desired and I refused for my desired to become dreams of the atmosphere.

Seeing glimpses of how my life could be continued fuel my energy for sacrifices. I began giving up things I loved – shopping, manicures, pedicures, steaks and social outings – to utilize those funds to build my dreams. I chuckle when people ask me how I could give up so much just for the POSSIBLITY of becoming successful. They often wonder why I laugh when I'm responding, it is merely because all of the premature sacrifices were preparation for those to come. The untold and Not . Posted sacrifices shaped me for bigger and better . . was it easy? You know the answer by now . . but it was worth it.

"In the midst of sacrifice, lean on the strength and endurance that life has already equipped you with. The simple things you may have to give up may very well be the keys to getting up"

5 OPTIMISIM
HOPEFULNESS AND CONFIDENCE ABOUT THE FUTURE OR THE SUCCESSFUL OUTCOME OF SOMETHING.

Optimism is often in a long-term battle with its evil twin or crazy cousin, whichever relation floats your boat, named Peter Pessimistic. Pessimism and pessimistic points of view often strongly overshadow those of optimistic nature. Why is this so? Well, let's just be honest, being optimistic, having high hopes and confidence can be draining. When the storms are raging and it seems as if nothing can go right, it is easy to lose sense of being optimistic

Being introduced to optimism early in life can have a very lasting impact on well-being and longevity, however statistics show it isn't as commonly instilled in the minds of young people. In the African American community primarily, it is more common for anger and negative attitudes to be exposed to children opposed to happiness and genuine positivity. It's not every home and it's not always on purpose; it's actually a learned systematic reaction to issues that most don't even realize.

Let's revert to a child living in one of our "what happens in this house, stays in this house" environments. Let's just say the child decided to expose what happened to them to a family member or friend. At this point the child has opened a window of vulnerability. The child has now been placed in a situation where something can be done or life can go on. In the worst case scenario that life just goes on, how do you think optimism is effected?

How is that child supposed to develop a sense of positive thinking?

On the same lines, what if that child is being reared by an adult that experienced tough circumstances in life and never let it go. There is a higher chance that optimistic thinking isn't prevalent in the home and as previously stated, it may not be recognized. When negative like thinking is systematically instilled, it takes work to transition to a positive mindset. Well you can't work on what you don't realize. Furthermore, depending on the magnitude, they may not believe in positivity.

Year after year, difficult things happen. Loss of jobs, houses, vehicles, loved ones – children not abiding to rules – friends betraying and walking away. How in the world can one tap into a spirit of optimism? Is it one of those dreams of the atmosphere that will never be attained. . . Though it often seems that way, it doesn't have to be. If you made it through whatever difficult situations life presented, there is a reason to be optimistic, you survived something!

I know you don't need this –light chuckle—but allow me to share three steps to shifting your mindset before I go into my personal reflection. There are several ways to cultivate the shift, I just happen to really like the ones I chose to share. I've seen them work miracles in my life and the life of others.

1. **Understand that perception is reality** – if you continue to think negatively on the behalf of your life, your surroundings, your future – your

outcomes will be just as you thought. Don't allow yourself to fall victim of the Peter Pessimistic way of thinking. For every action there is a reaction, allow your reactions to reflect positivity despite the original action. Additionally, your thoughts have impact on those around you – don't be the one that nobody wants to be around due to your negative energy.

2. **Give some attention to what's going well –** even when it seems like absolutely nothing is going well, find something to be grateful for. You're alive, you're in your right mind and you've completed 75% of this memoir. That's three right there! I challenge you each morning to identify three things that are going well in spite of all that isn't going so well. It's possible, do it!

3. **Watch Your Surroundings –** who are you allowing to pour into you? It is human nature to be influenced by those who are closest to us. No, no, no just because Uncle Peter Pessimistic or Cousin Patty Pessimistic is in your family, it doesn't mean you have to reflect their negativity. You do however have to make the decision on the amount of time you allow people such as these fictional family members to be around you. Often times the outpour of your optimism can cause others to shift, or at least not be negative around you. Other times it doesn't and you have to make the decision on the priority place they have in your life. As with most of the things I've

presented . . is it easy? Nah. Is it worth it? Of course! Your well-being matters!

These three steps are a jumpstart to optimistic thinking 365, optimistic thinking in spite of what's going on or what happens. The art of seeing positive outcomes despite turmoil or terrifying circumstances. Once you accept the challenge to shift, you will see a shift in many aspects of life. Things that once drove you crazy won't even have an effect. Things that once easily angered or aggravated you, won't even alter you attitude. Allow optimism to outpour into your daily thought process and witness magic happen.

A GLIMPSE OF THE UNTOLD: OPTIMISM

Optimism, one of the most beautiful aspects of my little life. Why so you ask? Oh because the journey to embody an optimistic spirit was just as tough or tougher than any other journey. Being a Nasty AND Negative Nancy would have been easier, likewise it would have been comforting to sink into the character of Patty Pessimistic. In all I've been through, it is no explanation as to how I can still be optimistic. Faith got me over, it's what worked for me, it's what fueled my shift.

From princess to poverty, from home with parents to where will I be tomorrow, from "normal" to "what in the world is going on". From fighting silent battles to becoming a minor victim of circumstances and knocking on the door of becoming a statistic. Shifting to an optimistic mindset was very difficult however it was one of the only things that saved my life at times.

Realizing that if I thought I could, I could. Realizing that positive thinking, yields positive actions which yields positive reactions from the atmosphere. Finding that peace and understanding through optimism could be a sword for all the battles.

I was about 19 years old, working 60-75 hours a week while matriculating through undergrad and trying to survive. To find positivity in the storm was hard, I often wondered "why me". Somehow with faith and optimistic thinking, the "why me" shifted to "why not me". With all I had been through in the previous 10 years, a little hard work and sacrifice of sleep couldn't break me. Holding firm that the current couldn't and wouldn't be the forever; kept pushing.

The more optimistic I tried to become it seemed as if oppression would dial my number a little more. I simply ignored the call and keep pushing, responding with a mindset of "you can't and won't stop me". Often fatigued from lack of sleep, often worried for I was so distant from my mother during times of illness, often feeling as if I should've given up – the negative thoughts didn't just disappear – I just had to deter them from taking over my mind.

Even now, pessimism is all around, people are always wondering what I'm doing, why I'm doing it and challenging my process. Thank all heavens for optimism and strong sense of self, I simply ignore it and keep moving. My life, my journey, my process isn't ideal for Peter Pessimistic because anything that isn't of the normal doesn't register in the mind of the negative. "Girl you need to sit down", "Why are you always with those kids, is it that serious", "Why do you travel so much, what do you have going on". The list goes on and on, it's actually pretty interesting. As crazy as it may sound, I enjoy listening to it. The energy helps to strengthen my optimistic mindset, furthermore it fuels me to keep on pushing. I have no plans to rub success in anyone's face; however those same folks are wondering how in the world great things just continue to happen. What you put in the atmosphere is what is returned unto you; I'm proof!

> *"Even when things aren't well, believe well and well will come. Optimism will assist you in creating opportunities, pessimism will cultivate and keep difficulties . .*
> *Adapt to what you want to adopt"*

NOT POSTED

6 NEGLECT
FAIL TO CARE FOR PROPERLY.

Transitioning from optimism and happy place to neglect is quite quirky, however isn't that how life works, you never know what you're going to get! You can go from smooth sailing to rocky roads in the blink of an eye. In the final phases of the season, I would be remised to leave out such a critical element.

Neglect – neglected feelings, neglected situations, neglected people – abandonment has many levels. Our child who has been traveling with us through the season has most likely faced neglect in some form or fashion, maybe multiple aspects of neglect. As with everything else, this is going to have a lasting impact on life as that child transitions into adulthood. Whatever happened that nobody saw fit to discuss and dissect is bottled up, emotional neglect. This is now going to impact self-worth and meaningfulness, am I enough? Do I matter?

In the news, neglect and abuse typically go hand and hand. In life, neglect and abuse correlate as well – to be neglected rather it be physically abandoned or emotionally alone, it is abusive to mindset and well-being. The neglected child becomes more prone to be the adult who accepts neglect in relationships both platonic and intimate because it is the norm. If it is never introduced that something different exists, what's familiar will seem like what is right.

Have you ever felt neglected? By family? Friends? Significant Other? Did you answer no . . . great, keep reading so that you can potentially see life through the eyes of others. Did you answer yes . . . how did it make you feel? Were you empty? Did you feel less than human? Now comes the real questions . . how did you cope? Did you really cope or did you adapt to the situation? Another real question, do we really know what neglect is? Hhhmm. . . Let's stick with our list of three thing from the last excerpt; after reading my spin on the classifications of neglect maybe you will be able to identify if any of these correlate with aspects of your past or current life.

1. **Emotional Neglect** – emotional neglect relates directly to having your emotional well-being treated with no care and given no attention. Often, emotional neglect occurs in the lives of children. Maybe parents work too much or have insecurities from their own childhood resulting in disconnect to emotional support. Maybe one or both parents are absent from the home entirely. Things such as these have an impact on emotional neglect, even if someone else gives the child attention and love in place of the parent(s).

    How many times were you asked how your day was? What you thought about things such as home improvement projects? The groceries? Relationships? Your future?

    It is my hope that you were asked about some of these things. If you weren't it is my hope that you ask others. Not just your children or young people, but also your friends, family and colleagues. You never know how my much it can help someone just to know that someone cares.

2. **Neglect by Ignoring** – Neglect by ignoring occurs when certain people, places and things are simply ignored due to personal choice or influence. People often think that ignoring something makes it just go away. In reality, ignoring anything does not make it go away though you may ignore it so long that in your mind you forget or block its existence. That sibling, aunt, cousin, old friend that you got into an altercation with and just decided to forget. You never talked about the issue or worked towards coming to common ground, the situation was merely ignored. Thus meaning, neither of you sincerely healed or let it go, it just "disappeared".

Ignoring situations such as when someone you love hurt your feelings or even to the magnitude of sexual or physical abuse. The individual(s) involved may have apologized or threatened you to be silent, therefore you never said anything. You moved on, you ignored the pain. I am not saying if this approach is right or wrong as this is definitely not my topic of "expertise". I will say however, the more you ignore, the more it impacts your life. You may become angered as a result, you may respond to situations differently because of the silence. Even if the day has come and gone and it's too late to address the situation, let it go in your mind, for you to be a better you.

3. **Neglect due to Ignorance** – I chose to address this one last as the previous two can happen as a

cause-and-effect to neglect due to ignorance. Neglect due to ignorance occurs when the person(s) neglecting their child, significant other, family or friends is completely unaware of their actions. This is the most common form of neglect being that many carry over the character traits that they learned or observed in their lives. If neglect was prevalent in the home growing up, you are more prone to neglect as second nature. Being ignorant to the fact. Just as this is the most common, it is the most difficult to identify and deal with. We are creatures of habit by nature therefore what feels comfortable is what we do.

Though there is no excuse for neglect; neglect by ignorance is so out of sight, out of mind, that it is unethical to place to fault all on the "neglector". The neglect may be so deeply rooted into the family that the fault can be rerouted backwards for generations. With all that being said . . . Who's darn fault is it? AND, how can we change it?

Who? Well that I can't quite coin how to identify, let's not event try. Let's take the effort and apply it to deriving how to work on change. We must work on being more observant and attentive. We can't just assume that just because something has been done the same way for so long that it is correct. Furthermore, we cannot allow our past to overshadow our futures and the magnitude of influence we can have on those around us. Embrace the things that hurt you and identify times where you were neglected. Allow yourself to cope with and move pass these situations so that you can be of a caring nature to others.

So . . . now that we have had our short "knowledge on neglect" session, it is my hope that you will take these nuggets and work towards not being a "neglector". Support and show care for those who are in your direct and indirect circles. Allow it to be known that you are there. You never know when you are the only one who has done such a thing.

A GLIMPSE OF THE UNTOLD: NEGLECT

Since I am not a fan of the word "lucky" I will go on a whim and say I was blessed in the early years of my life. I was far from neglected. My feelings and opinions were taken into consideration from the time I was able to speak. My parents and grandparents would have actual conversations with me to ensure I understood certain aspects of life. Before the many forms of "what happens in this house, stays in this house" took over, I had no idea what it felt like to be neglected. I always knew someone was going to ask my opinion about food, school, clothes, my small little savings account (which I am so glad I had, learned a lot very early), the games I played and the list goes on.

Well when life went from princess to poverty – neglect was allllllll around. Nobody inquired about how I felt about my parents having to separate. Nobody asked how it felt to be snatched from my home leaving behind many things that impacted my childhood to be moved from place to place. Not a soul thought it was necessary to talk to me – possibly because I was kid or possibly because they were neglecting by ignorance. I find peace in processing that none of the adults I was around knew how to deal with what was going on, everyone was just doing the best they could. For that reason and that reason alone, I was able to let my anger go.

My mother was ill, who I knew to be my father was miles away and my grandparents were aging. My fabulous four couldn't help me and I felt so all alone. There were family members who stepped up to the plate to ensure I was alive and well to their standards however no real mental or emotional support existed. Neglect by ignoring. We are just going to ignore that all these traumatic things are occurring in the child's life before she's even 10. We will just make sure she has a place to stay, clothes, food and can go to school. As you can now probably relate, this is where that exerting of energy through attitude that we discussed earlier came from. With so many bottled up issues and neglect in every form – something had to be my escape from reality. Yes I had an attitude, but at least I was alive which was in itself a step.

For many years, I let the hurt that came from neglect haunt me. I did not want to be around anyone who played a role in "caregiving" for me while my mother was ill. I was angry that they did not do more, say more, ask more. During my phase of "recreating Tap" I had to forgive them, I had to conceptualize with what I said earlier: they did the best they could.

As a result of neglect, I became a "neglector" in a sense. I would neglect to acknowledge certain situations that occurred as they were painful. I neglected to share how I really felt. I became so accustomed to not trusting others and believing that nobody genuinely cared that I would just keep things to myself and see it through alone. Always seeking guidance from above but never allowing earthly individuals to be of assistance. I am working to become better on this aspect but it is definitely a process. Told y'all, we are creatures of habit and that's one of my habitual ways of dealing.

In my relationships and friendships, I find myself becoming over caring as a result of not having that. I often ask a lot of questions and desire to know that those I love are "okay". The issue with this is . . . for me to love, it takes a lot. The inability to trust creates a subconscious barrier for me block people out. Another thing that is being worked on. Not that I want to trust and love any and everybody, I just don't want to automatically block people due to effects of a troubled past.

Needless to say, I was intentional beyond the fact that "N" is the last letter of the word SEASON. Leaving this excerpt and the items addressed within it was purposeful. Neglect is a touchy subject for me as I know it is for many. It is difficult to know that those we love may have done things that have impacted our well-being and life trajectory. Together we can overcome, we can forgive those who have no idea what they've done and we can . . . let . it . go!

"A neglected wound will never heal. Apply care, apply love and apply understanding and watch the would slowly diminish to an unrecognizable size."

"We can become so lost in what went wrong that we neglect to appreciate what went right. If we continue as such, all will be wrong and no right will be present"

"A happy birthday can go a long way to someone who has never heard one. An I love you can save a life for someone who's never heard the phrase. Be intentional in your words, you may be interacting with a survivor of severe neglect"

NOT POSTED

BONUS
7 SOCIAL PERCEPTION

HOW PEOPLE FORM IMPRESSIONS OF AND MAKE INFERENCES ABOUT OTHER PEOPLE.

Well we made it through the season, good job. It is my hope that through the excerpts addressing strength, endurance, attitude, sacrifice, optimism and neglect you learned something or refreshed your current knowledge on something. From my personal glimpses into the untold moments, it is my hope that my untold aspects empowered you, inspired you and enlightened you on how it is definitely possible to overcome. Additionally, it is okay to be transparent. Keeping everything in can be a killer; literally, check the rates, self-harm and suicide as a result of holding issues in happens daily.

Okay so the "S" is here, good ol' social perception. The way we are perceived by people based on the things they see and hear as it relates to us. Social perception is often so far off from a person's real identity that is hard to believe once you ever meet the real person. The World Wide Web and social media have had an impact on social perception however people were making character assumptions far before the internet or computers.

Social perception correlates directly with the "you" that people see. The majority of the time you have no control over how people perceive you for the perception is created in their mind utilizing their thought process.

It's example time – I pull up in a new car and get out with nice clothes, shoes and accessories. The first perception some may derive is wealth, another person may think debt, another person may not form any prejudgments and just keep moving. The social perception formed is going to vary based on the person observing and the way they characterize individuals.

A girl in her twenties gets out of a car with four children. One may perceive her as promiscuous, one may perceive her as a struggling young mother and one may wonder if she was forced into motherhood. Another set of three differing perceptions.

From these two examples, think of the many ways you are perceived based on what others see. Furthermore, think of how you perceive others. If you utilize social media, think about how it plays a role in perception. Often times, before we can even think that people post what they want, the highlights, the filtered image, we imply perceptions on their life.

Brand new car – ooouuu somebody has money, but do they? Engagement or new relationship – ooouuu they're in love, but are they? Are they just doing it for the people? Good grades, why can't I do it? Did you think about the sacrifice they made for those grades? The extra hours they may have put in to obtain such academic achievement. . . These are just a few examples, the list goes on and on.

It is so funny to me that when I first began to develop this piece, it was heavy rooted in social media and social perception. How did I change gears? Well I didn't really – when you think about it everything we talked about comes full circle to conclude with this excerpt on social perception.

People make characterizations on you based on social perception but what would they think if they knew just a bit of your untold stories? Not all, like I told you earlier, I am not at all advising you to let all the bats out of the closet, however I am asking you to be more open, more transparent, more unfiltered in nature. Even if it's not with the world let it be with your household. Don't allow your household to suffer because of your past experiences. Don't be so succumbed by the social perception that you fall victim to not knowing or loving yourself.

If nothing else from this memoir registers, I want you to understand that you too can empower with the untold story. Rather you change one person's life or 1,000 people's lives – you can do it! Do it for you, do it for your well-being and do it for those who have to be around you.

"It is very difficult to see things as they are, it is easier for us to see things as we are. Challenge yourself to think beyond self, there is a world that expands beyond our "norm", embrace it"

S.E.A.S.O.N.S. of the Untold

STRENGH
ENDURANCE
ATTITUDE
SACRIFICE
OPTIMISM
NEGLECT
SOCIAL PERCEPTION

Thank you for journeying with me through the S.E.A.S.O.N.S. of the Untold – be inspired to empower with your untold story.

Conclusion
UNTIL WE MEET AGAIN, YES, WE WILL MEET AGAIN

I had a blast composing this through all the ups and downs of making it possible. It is my hope that it will be a vessel for you to move beyond some of the untold things that have held you back before. You may go on to write a letter, a paper, a memoir or even a book to express your feelings. You may begin to talk to your family and friends about how things have impacted you. Whatever it is that you chose, chose it and embrace it. Empower yourself and others with the untold story.

Have a story in mind that you want to share or know someone who has untold aspects of their life that they are itching to share with the world? Well hold tight but get ready. In January 2018, I will open a call for submissions for my next memoir. It will be a collection of untold stories and how people of various walks of life overcame. I will have a team of reviewers to assist me in selecting 10-15 stories to be published Summer 2018.

Until we meet again, be inspired, be empowered and whatever is holding you back from doing so . . .Let. It. Go!

S.H.E. thought She could, so She did.

ABOUT THE AUTHOR

Tabitha D. James "Tiny Tab", is a native of the rural South. She is originally from Lake View, SC, a very small town located about 45 miles north of the tourist destination Myrtle Beach. She can be classified as an entrepreneur, educator, facilitator, philanthropist, life-learner, woman of God and several other things as it relates to her accolades; however she is not the biggest fan of titles.
She is simply and authentically herself, a humble servant.
A **S**urvivor, **H**elping to **E**mpower.

www.tabithadjames.com

www.ingramcontent.com/pod-product-compliance
Lightning Source LLC
LaVergne TN
LVHW051528070426
835507LV00023B/3374